Creature

Rosalee Kiely

Creature

Acknowledgements

I wish to thank the editors of the following publications, in which some of the poems in this collection have previously appeared: *ANU Writer's Block, Australian Poetry Journal, dotdotdash, Rabbit, Regime* and *Voiceworks*.

Some of these poems appeared in a joint exhibition *Away from Home* with Gabriela Morales at Bank Street Arts in Sheffield, UK, in 2016.

My heartfelt thanks to the late Judith Rodriguez, the Moat/Yak poets, Jacinta Le Plastrier, Irene, John, Erica, Jack, Noah, Gaby and all my friends and family.

Special thanks to Richard Ford for his kind permission to quote from his short story 'Great Falls'.

Creature
ISBN 978 1 76041 677 5
Copyright © text Rosalee Kiely 2019
Cover image: Golden retriever dog hair, by tevalux11
'Great Falls' from *Rock Springs* by Richard Ford. Published by Grove, 1987. Copyright © Richard Ford. Reproduced by permission of the author c/o Rogers, Coleridge & White Ltd, 20 Powis Mews, London W11 1JN

First published 2019 by
GINNINDERRA PRESS
PO Box 3461 Port Adelaide 5015
www.ginninderrapress.com.au

Contents

Lines	9
The Best of Montana's Short Fiction	10
Huntsman	12
Halifax	13
Walk Beside Salt Water	14
Leaving Land	15
Snow Fruit	16
Lesson	18
Year	19
Beograd Railway Station	21
Wrecks	22
If Love is a Line on the Ocean	23
Father	25
Painting in a Restaurant	26
Banksia	27
Winter Dream	28
Why I Write	30
After All	31
Homecoming	32
Moon Verses	35
I Would Send This In Your Gentle Time	36
Glacier	38
Lunch Break	39
On Moving	41
Sisters	43
Ferry	44
Job Seeker	45
What the Crack Lets In	47
Summer Night	48
Same Bay	49

Foxes	50
Song	52
My Mother Was a Missionary	53
Learning To Love You More	55
Night Walk	58
Greyhound	59
The Canyon	60
Pocket	61
Summer Rain	63
Notes on Poems	64

I have seen my mother from time to time – in one place or another, with one man or other – and I can say, at least, that we know each other…

It is just low-life, some coldness in us all…makes us no more or less than animals who meet on the road.

Richard Ford, *Great Falls*

Lines

for Erica

We fished at Coffin Bay with hand reels
on a chalky ledge
playing fishing with grey air
expecting nothing

spilling forth
at our feet for once
when I pulled my fish
the only fish we took.

(Another time much later
with you
when you were in your raw bones
we dragged a lure
quicksilver
behind a motorboat.)

But then I carried my fish myself
in a skin-thin shopping bag.
Dad gutted it like a tourist
giddy with life it tasted good.

The Best of Montana's Short Fiction

when you leave the train the air is slushy with cold
at the Whistlestop Café you eat
a slice of huckleberry pie
there are
the fine-pocked mountains
lakes green with rock dust
the tufted forest
and water gushing melt from every crevice
and water gorging the trail
with every gone sheet of ice
and later
the big throw quilt sky

oh beautiful.

on the train you read stories
the cover shows a woman in paisley
poised at the doorway of a van
what face she must have had

looked into those mountain-wrecks
of thaw, avalanche, gravel slide
a board by the highway: Best-Margaritas
Cook-Required

so the stories as you moved
made real feeling people in the mountains
beneath the big sky and I
far from Montana
farther still from home myself
saw something at least in a land that took
all people willing to witness their life
knifed to the open
sinew and raw
and only solace in wild places to ease heartache.

Huntsman

'The heart is a lonely hunter' – Carson McCullers

hunter in a glance dislocates himself: hair weft to flesh
flesh the sleeve caught
on a nail
the nail the shock
in a mirror of one's face

started upright by a paddock gate
with a gun on the shoulder in effigy
of a man wrenched and fixated on the silk of his mind.
the abject disfigurement of man

recoils from his strangeness
the pocket of night turned inside out.

still, tendrils of dawn change the sky
the plinths of feet crackle with frost
a seed grows roots in his chest

then, two boots walk the world home
unlace together and unbutton the clothes
skin, hair, bones lie down, bent to the other one
the faces a mirror, the breath warming chinks to the pillow.

Halifax

When I lived with strangers
we left tomato
on the floor for a month

the harbour smoked on cold
days we crossed sheets of ice
to the supermarket

we took tequila with lemon in
salty plastic cups that eased
nothing so much as

when I lived with you

snow fell for the orange night
I pulled my bones
across the wind-hauled street

you spun me to pop songs
in a Pacific-themed nightclub
our

soles felt earth through
ruptured snow and always
you said stay close.

Walk Beside Salt Water

twist up in sails your hurricane mind
scramble, grind your palm away

until the gum fallen from the forest will touch
the sea – boys fish there
together with their shy voices
and bait box.

when eventide parcels up in smoke
a fisherman on the water takes his boat
across the bay in changing heart.

go up the sand path
drawn by a moth's longing not for light
but darkness made sharpest
by light.

after all she decides: fear
simple and heavy as the anchor
of shame
the marzipan sludge in a buggered
artery

of wildfire wasting to bone
the intense glow of red on water in
the nub of a stone on the shore.

Leaving Land

Leaving land for black waste beneath
a sheen of a steaming lake
the water smells of spent leaves on such a night
ringed by low trees as we strike off our clothes
and make for the pontoon in the middle.

Or at least this is how I imagine it
years later. What we did was take
the canoe to a platform where they
told me this was a forest custom
that I don't have to join in
if I don't want to
then she and he were naked and diving
into the smoky deep
and making out while I swam

stupid circles. It was spring, the water
warm, full of promise and
frogs and insects singing
all along
so I slipped off my bathers
and swam towards shore.

Snow Fruit

Wonder, season's snow
fledged in cool-box of air
warms into the tall earth
molten in plant feet, falling

drops and veins from the
named and unnamed hills
calling down to meet water
droplets of all the mountains

by fast rivers a drain
incises the ground to a lake
falls by dam and
a dam

the click of an oarlock
in hill-deep tunnels
inland to straight cuts
green as Eden on a bone.

Wonder, the river
blasted by thumbs against
every gravity, winces
an allocation

into its own valley, ghost-worn
by relentless spring
explosions, droplet rally
en masse to sea. Or the scour

ends in fruit. Rub an apple
on your sleeve.
Bite. Ahead everything
is decided

but there, in snow
do not underestimate a tunnel
weir, turbine, station, switch.
The mystery is what they cannot hold.

Lesson

if I practised love
buoyed by the secret
in your wooden kitchen

upstairs the moon
in relief through the glass
slipped to separation

until moon lives in the room
and trains pass by
and the roof covered your bed.

if I practised wonder
for you on the doorstep
baptised in chequered shorts

or at night where the street
dipped and the houses were unlit
one kiss you turn

then all I learnt
would portend
your stamp on my heart
pretend, or pretend.

Year

when it was winter
I didn't live
without the breath of you.
on the stair lacing your feet
we'd never met
you talk so gentle. I'd seen myself
but never you:
blue-coal eyes from the stair.

when it was summer
you were a sun-blush drink I
wasted myself on in quiet rooms
or reverie amidst chatter
not you the one on the stair
but you who I'd
made.

there was rain that year
floods all over the news
a teenage hero saw his mum
freaking out, told her
he thought she was doing a good job.
the bay went brown with muck
almost orange, they said.
where a week ago in desiccated heat

I'd swum at midnight and flung
from still water the glow
-in-the-dark
of phosphorescence

landed in luminous tears.
over and over I rummaged the skin
of the bay and the ruptures were

more wonderful than all the street lights
any light winkling on the far side.

Beograd Railway Station

he called 'Hey, what's wrong?'
so I sat on the bench
thinking a person could change
a petite, everlasting vine
might here close and also open

time into wax, wax into runner
like the immense hammer
that bangs out an etching of a girl.
were there foxes?
he said not. his photos cascaded
like a waterfall, river to the sea
sweeping along its buoy.

his offence started when I
wouldn't travel with him
when the trains cleaved cells
edging the eyelet of velvet ribbon
he went home to movies
home to his own heart.
and so did I.

Wrecks

after the storm we go to the beach.
we see how the sea has moved stone
and broken up concrete and where exactly
the sea was ferocious.
the sea is flat now.
another day we walked into a gallery
to see the floor all over life vests
twisted, ribbons flaring, white.
a guide tells a group the vests
are marble. carved to life from marble
they are vests of children and adults
laid waste before paint-smudged walls
an island.
and this, afterwards, and all in pieces
is not the wreck but the story of the wreck
desolation pared to the bones, *we are
I am, you are*, and if names do not appear
in the book of myths
if the myths are horrors and the sea is flat
in the end always the same
marble vests, heavy on the floor.

If Love is a Line on the Ocean

summer has already gone
trees keen to orange outside

sleepwalking the long road away
from a wonderful time of my life

for if love is a line on the ocean
there is my floating red heart

there is the match between safety and flame
the tip to my apple-green dart

and if a bird flies from the water
if a bird sinks in the night

I've pretty well left that behind me
to eat cast-away rations of nice

nice is a fish in the headlights
fish flashes belly to sun

a fish was ancient, and migrated
all her mothers fin-to-fin

to pelvic fin, fleet in the water
lantern fish dangling their lure

long-nosed garfish, schooling sardines
porcupine fish growing bones

down their sides, clown fish in corals
high flying fish, cross-country salmon

the ocean has places that drift
the places are world drowned in water

the wind was a song in the waves all along
so leave me your kippers for breakfast

leave your white blossoming bones
leave your dismay at the end of the day

and dine with me alone on the phone?

Father

What happened was the sunshine turned to one side
Blue shapes in a night time corridor.
Except the puzzle of coffee dregs and empty bottles
I took up the bottlebrush and worried out the spent sauce
Fastidiously recycled – defeated – but something had to keep going.
Because I'd seen you first, crowned with blood and vernix
Separating like a mushroom from your mother's body.
Your steel eyes looked the size of an expanding universe
Your bud-like toenails and miniature fist
And your magenta mouth split open with noise it never made before
And you gurgled out cries like scrapping kittens, horrified.
Then I honoured you above all else.

Your mother suckled you while she watched TV.
At night I walked you to the window to see the moon.
Your mother moved around the corner. I went there
To take you to the park in the stroller
Tight in your coat on the grass under the figs.
One day I went around you weren't there any more.
It took me seventeen months to find you.
The judge didn't like me. Your mother hated me.
Afterward my mother drove us from the court
You in your new seat very quiet, until you turned to me, said
'Daddy?'
And my mother kept driving.

Painting in a Restaurant

imagine this moon-child, when you're sad:

every night is different
a little more sun, a little less
until the full circle breathes into shadow villages.

you were blue before and the moon was your friend

you stood in its boat with flowers in your arms
you rowed through the sky
always upright
always looking to the bow

about the rocks
falling with inhuman fire

as you sailed through cloud
as you sailed through hair.

cut deeper and forget your sullen reflection

leaves on Earth only want to multiply
and the wood fire burns in you too
little camp fires in your cells

you could throw yourself down in flames
you could show the sun something else
when it looks back and sees specks of itself caught
in the universe

transfigured

Banksia

I lay between the roots of a banksia tree
in the season when the candles flame.

what made you come nearer and stay
when I wouldn't reveal a leaf of my mind.

the tablelands of daily and wooden amount.
a drop of nectar birds wrestle to get out.

Winter Dream

he has a logger's hair
pale at the roots
with bloodless privation

he says the difference now
is I talk with you
but won't raise anything.

he meant we were done
a short-sheeted bed.
fine, I said.

ruin softened him
and winter eyebrows
turned to snow

I thought that's what I saw.
on the mountain side
the gums cover air

and snow, an ersatz house.
the first poem I wrote
like ice from the tongue

of everything
between word, image
word a hair away

deeper, burrowed
the soul gets out
or suffocates

through lack.
a wishbone morning
earth tremor

rain in my shoe
meaning: scrabble,
scrabble, shrink.

or at the dock
I said everything.
he didn't speak.

the river is just grey
the sky just sky
when he said

I

still
think

about

you

I am laid waste
in the vein

Why I Write

Mice on a page scritch at the stones
I try to make a house of cards
And the bear makes floes on foolscap all white
Each card holds by a millimetre   less
And canary is for sky balloons

What you are exactly when you mean
We pick blue plums in summer
Notice stones that say glad or
Surfers bob as leaves pressed in paper
Forgiveness   You are this

Purple lupins grow by the fence on the cape
I write the house and if it stands I'm proud
It won't matter so much if it matters now
I write and maybe the world is blank
Your face is new as an infant's

From my bedroom the door is open
The moon rises like light to a
Tunnel or the yolk of an egg   There
Is hope to see it align with the street sign
In the trout-coloured sky between chimneys

After All

the stars are mapped in the sky these several years
the summer countryside yellow
solace makes me wonder, the gummed-up eaves
will rinse their steel rainwater
beauty is the thing that hooks the guts
I was afraid hundreds of times like a bone

that will not sing, except –

flooding it down the highway, saying nothing
the claim of his hand.

his hand, his hand.

Homecoming

I

Christmas Eve I water plants out the front
that seemed to die in dry months
but shoot now from grey sand.
water runs over, I cup and dam
to hold the water
to keep these plants, to shore the soil

soil I've seen slicked on the bottom path after rain
I've shovelled it back

the air shifting at sunset
something like a tower or a country
the sky vaulted by stars.

II

two days from Christmas the psychologist said
cry every day for five years if you need to: have faith.
then I went shopping in the city.
now the dairy maid is 97. her skin shreds up cabbage
shakes the broom over the lino
folds up under the bedside lamp to read a Cinderella novel
about the war. her painting's a forest after fire.
when she reads she's not painting.
she hauls linen through the wash and we lie reading
and she speaks in a fabric of chat that isn't to entertain
but to bind or hold, sturdier than liking.
it's awful not being able to hear.
birdsong, hens in only this garden.
sometimes just sitting, the room in flux.
we've prepared all day for this dinner.
I hadn't trusted myself to feel small.

III

out near the end of summer, the day is a clean, warm bone
the dog is wet from the sea, still wet
thick, seal wet, he carries the sea in his hair.

this is the wall my father walked along
the wall my mother and my father walked along
the wall my mother and my grandmother walked along
the wall the dogs walked along, and the benches and horizon
and the fisher people always there after dark in the middle of winter.

now my voice is the cracked road that goes past plain fences
and rose bushes, meaning it's all for show
so when I say it's peaceful, lovely, you understand only because
you are here too and see the gums dripping their leaves
into fringes all around us, tough, frail leaves
the overgrownness of my father's plants, their own devices creating
this effect, or privacy, or faraway

and the hill used to face Arthur's Seat chairlift
to flash on a clear day, across the bay
and there was a peach tree right there
but my grandmother painted the tree in bloom at least twice
so my father chopped it down
years later she touched it up, added some colour to the blossom
made the frame blue. the sea is blue today
we see it, we comment on the sea, that we see it.

later I'm down at the water, my lungs draw
at the cold, the horizon that peachiness of sunset.
it's glowing and the water is cold.

Moon Verses

travel with a full moon
a cycle turning
the pull and draw of waves
the winter between summer
the moon would say
or the wind has changed
the moon is naked tonight
awake and resilient in grip
in frost on the lawn
exhausted turn your mind
that what seems comfort
a ti-tree branch curves
the sorrow of paper
the moon was cold as butter and spread

you are not alone
the belt of seasons
of ripening fruit
between harvest
this hand
has found
its shadow
of dream
in the tap of feet
over each word
is only the hope
in a knot of sticks

and as I walked I was afraid.

I Would Send This In Your Gentle Time

I would send this in your gentle time
for vegetable hours creep viney and vast
down winter gardens to the clothesline
find a swollen hush and burst at last.

Like a time, my aunt with wine, my mother water
remembering their mother. I remember
only a game in a spare room
her caged canaries quickened with life

how we cried when sat on her lap, grapes
real and plastic, cigarettes
our own mother's day in bed
but how can something that happens be a mystery.

How to hear in the night an aircraft call
touch the weave of a slip, feel a camp ground
take a daughter on a liner and endure survival
in a limestone town by a far south ocean.

She raised her ducks in case of famine
their father, drunk, potted them off.
The Luke Street Massacre, they joked.
Now the aunt and my mother

laugh like two fiends from some place
where blackest humour can enter
grief at its deepest
so a hard memory is perceived

and into every green home day
threaded like a scaffold
with repetition and peace:
this happiness is sacred.

Glacier

go into the fern and moss
gathered, undilute
green in the rain out of town
and go past it.

go until the moonish flat
is marked by falls
veining the valley in rain
and gravel tracks

toward the glacier
slumped in its sleep-gouged
chamber, creature shrink
of retreat, fluttering

bloodlessness.
go where the melt menaces
grey water, bearing threat
bearing redemption.

Lunch Break

A gull pulled into her wings
could be on an Antarctic rock
or scooping over any river
through wilderness
cutting the density of treetops.

*

But today the end is silt from suburbs
and hills and calling school children
sure as the cold slide of a tram

then fallen leaves hurl
into the water

under green tide lines
hints of an office tower
the suggestion of brown leaf.

*

The torn windsock at the helipad
collects the wind, the clouds
fill the foot bones of buildings
and sewer holes with the smell of water.

*

Some thread of white is caught
and the tide is a hand from the scum line.
How to prepare for the weight of water
sliding into and over its own mud
the unseparateness of particles
and gulls and offices on a flood plain
a ferry cat and the airborne pieces of spume
ricochet languorous and the ebb, tide and slow

quiet anger of rivers sweeping low places
fair in volume and manoeuvring
of cans, soccer balls, dirt, sewage, reeds,
spinning flocculant with threaded fingers

overskated by scullers and kids in rings
and the foot soles of legs off a jetty
and called to sweep away everything
and not to look back or to think back
quick-stream, slow-stream, bay, ocean.

On Moving

Bougainvillea
wickered the sky
shed paper leaves

we hauled tarpaulin
rain funnelled
into the *clericot*

we argued about clothes pegs
then fussed hanging clothes
to stay away

soothed by
palm tree, cats
a star.

I am reminded by
one winter
that beside the garden

are the bricks we
lived between
when air was saturated

by cold or night
and the short pleasure
in outdoors expired

where we went to, ate
and lay down.
Soon time will gild

with distance
yet it was daily struggle
alloyed at points

like fingertips
coincided
the lightest, softest window.

Sisters

Were we a book club? We said No, there's just nothing left to say. We laughed. I expected things to return, birds to the nest, and if the same things were giddy, the ground underfoot had worked on us. We went to sea, to snow, we walked and ate, she had patience and no patience. I found the passage in a journal: *American landscape, fierce and sublime*; the poems a water music clean as ice, plain as water (but less dangerous).

Newport Beach: scene of our worst argument, she hit me so I hit her, on the boardwalk marching along to Flo's Clam Shack, the cold spring sun, a pile of clam cakes neither of us liked. Somehow New York again, Montreal, Toronto, the last night raining, a Chinese place outside China Town, the menu, and all the things we said that were true and are true though I've forgotten what they are. It's true that sisters fight and in a magazine profile I read, sisters do move around the world to leave, just to get away. My dark mirror, my piece and my part.

Ferry

when to stop
begins seam
lessly

a trout belly

at sea
the membrane
of horizon

splits water
from air
less certain

than a

shark embryo
heartbeats in a
backlit egg

breathing

volition
alone
ruthless

and ignorant:
desire
and nothing else.

Job Seeker

Coles and Woolies, Coles and Woolies
every fortnight – her lipstick bleeds

to the hairline cracks of a town
knotted into strings of a fishing industry

and outside the industrial net / fish who won't get fat

who drink all day, won't work, won't try
won't even leave, because everyone agrees

there's no opportunity / there: if a town could break off from a rock

and land in a jewel of sea, barren and mirage-like

there are the mansions up the hill
the guard dogs drawing their teeth on fence lines.

if there are no jobs and there's no hope / and there's drink and babies
but down at the swimming shed

those babies are getting changed / crystal water ahead

and the tuna are fat, spray fed notes of fish meal
looping the net, strata on strata, gorging, fattening fishies

until they *do* leave / ice blocks, Japan, *John West*.
She sees the farms from her mid-hill window

flattened, clumped in the bay, tended by boat-shapes
that come and go, come and go

boats telling their fish, stay, get fat, make us money we don't care it's all work

land out of town wasn't arable, became a National Park
enriched by machinery rusting

in town there's a marina, hotel on the beach
airport, a cemetery, silos, there's still Miss Tunarama

those houses where people used to live
in the shabby part of town / and the farms up close

are huge, fierce and flashing under the weight of confined meat
everyone can see opportunity's already there.

What the Crack Lets In

the plum or not the plum.
but not the crimson skin, the give of skin
the tang sweet filaments cling to stone
the plum stone laid on china.

the memory or not the memory.
but not the taste of ashes, writing a name
in ashes
and not the grief of ashes
the loss of arms, chest, dwelling.

the road or not the road.
but not the seat by the road
the dirty, weary limbs tapping time
and not the splendour and sickness for home
the driver saying God bless our souls.

perfection or not perfection.
but not the water rising in one vent
and not the breath
the trust in hair or music, and not
crying by the line, sink, bed
and not the grace and not the courage.

Summer Night

on the oval sprinklers
twirl puny arms on
the parched pitch.

the house lolls humid air
I crave outside like
a swimmer wants sea.

my hair shakes salt, flakes
of so much salmon.
a flower

has opened its scent
into everything.
milk, honey and now hunger.

Same Bay

The pink hibiscus
bloomed all over the chook pen
and the dog sleeps like a standing dog
turned to his side, but the teenage boys curl up
in the slow burn of a slow afternoon.

In the newspaper, the water drained out to reveal
which swimmers were naked.
The familiar house the refuge
in its bones that you forgot about
and can't read anything into, except the news
of the shooting, a great leaking eye.

The beach on the same bay: white flecked waves, green sea.
White, broken crests, yellow buoys
the pale blue sky and the red-hulled boat
and cream shins and green waves
marbled with foam and a storm-hulled boat
and pale blue horizon and yellow umbrellas
and sand.

This lesson in what I have, falling apart.
This lesson on the wind in my bones, falling apart
this wind in my skirt, in my bones.
What was left, incredible, without form
boundless

Foxes

It looks like I've got no skin, said the fox
the moon leaned in

and it sailed through hair
so the clouds made a coat and the fox
was a droll heeled thing, a pig in overalls
fancy that.

At the beach on the sand
running from water to cliff, the darkened shore
edge of light, shadow and edge, a fox

because in this cubicle of light and dark is such a stuck prism
such a this or that.

Please like me, said the fox with its teeth
the moon rose like grief

for the red meat on the rib cage, but it's more simple
it's very simple and in a language I do not know.

Wily, mysterious thing, more cat, more dog?
Something English slinking from the hedgerows.

My parents joined a weeding group
the story of a lady who fed foxes there
she was seen, the skirted lady
food from her pockets in the dark or dawn

ranged by dark or light figments of
bush – unreleased by fire
wasteland of blackberry we forever hacked away on Sundays.

I didn't know you could feed foxes
or that taming exists, by daily act.
I didn't know you could grow up to feed foxes.

Song

*I've thought so many stories, it's like the wind breathes
when one comes, the other goes away.*

*And I've woven threads to castles in the house's
frail dawn*

*and nothing's come to anything, zero's in the dust
the spinning faces, flowers tear.*

*I won't be happy, I won't be sad.
Give me bare bones, any day.*

My Mother Was a Missionary

A nun blessed her
and said *Pray*, so she did
over a worry cleaved to
the Pacific feet
pressed beneath crushing water
blue sky and sharp light
the hanging question
and she tasted or felt
altogether knew
that belief or non-belief
are the same.

I've seen the slides
projected onto our dim wall
the shy smile
already 'sway' back
wreath of flowers in cropped hair
everything so bright
the shadows are black:

he had an affair with her
sometimes we flew to another island
she stopped writing last year
there was the teachers' quarter
our cats, the Sister I liked
the toilets over the sea
the woven churches, the cloth they wore
tied this way at the waist
and three years, much
too
long.

So it *was* a miracle
or at least, before I knew this story
she said she did believe
something had happened once
that made her believe.
It was just this.
It was enough.

In a purely cool
mist-draped evening
in green-belt suburbia
free of our cavernous share house
when trees creak
the horizon toward the city glows velvet brown
of geriatric pets, consider
the capacity to love
in the message
consider the answer
irrelevant.

Learning To Love You More

she was my room-mate in the dorm
I was tearing my hair out
she asked me to dinner.

afterwards we walked across the big square
in front of the cathedral and stopped
to watch a *tuna* music group

romancing the late crowd
with their bawdy lawyer revue.
they asked my friend to dance

and she being a fun girl
danced and I took photos for
her boyfriend.

afterwards I followed her
and the men up an alley to their dressing room
and drank some beers

and listened to their Spanish
and waited for someone to notice me
or the moment I could sleep

but we went to an empty bar instead and
played electronic darts and the barmaid
knew them and some of them spoke English

one of the men tried to kiss me
I pushed him away because he was
almost too young

but I already wanted him to
so we went to a booth in an alcove
I lost a drop earring

and when it was time to go I said I
was coming back to the hostel with my friend
then she took me to the bathroom

and asked me what I really wanted
she said it's not like he's a stranger
I've never done it before either though

so we left the bathroom and I said ok
I'm coming with you
one of his friends patted my arm

we all set off, his guitar over shoulder
the old streets were quiet as stone
when we split away he didn't take my hand

he asked me what my room-mate said
I said she said nothing.
in the apartment he steered me in the dark

to the bathroom with hands on my hips
I found my way to the sofa.
he took off his funny high shoes

his baggy jacket with the puff sleeves
I asked him to close the blinds
he locked the door and we took our clothes off.

I thought it would hurt but it didn't
he turned the light on and lit a cigarette
and covered himself with an ashtray.

a few hours later I could not wake him
I've never seen a man with hips before
he didn't get up to walk me to the hostel

some of his girl housemates were eating breakfast.
I got lost going back
but found my way. later a woman

ran from a fruit and cheese shop without paying
everyone looked shocked.
I left my room-mate a note with my email

saying I'd email her the photos.
I had bruises on my neck for a few days.
later I told a friend I wanted to see if I could

and it was like nothing. it was no big deal.

Night Walk

in the desert of brambles and thorns
our skin was like plastic

scrabbling into dregs of hope, omens
we cut loose from home

kids doing surgery on capillaries
pulling out awful lengths

onto the tar beneath trees
into the milk of limbs

into the solid face of moon in the leaves
we strode together, drank it in.

Greyhound

my life unravels on a string
water memory, tissue moon.

dream and time dissolve my chest
oar-lights on highway lever the bus

to the spare room ahead.
wake to a kettle of housekeeping

outside grapple at berry canes
of remembering, a bone chill

cloud weighted to the ground
I wake, it is just the season:

grass, persimmon, whey
or loam

for now the trinkets are turned
the table an old wooden table

the lean-back couch a dusty thing
my mum and dad look like they sit

reading when I come in, and now I know
home has fled until I make my own.

The Canyon

by some trick she broke the ordinary loaf
one part, the pinch of morning sun
of afternoon

everything is washing past.
ahead on the current, thin
in the phantom water
is another country, the ice
uncrushed and quick, almost white.
there will always be this solace: this chance of an arm
and what was left, the world in pieces.
life wins, always.

the last tiny stone of fig bitterness
the bitter, warm fig milk
when we left it was slowly, snips across a plain, we hoped
and were gone, strangers in a strange land
and the familiar could not be conjured back

our daily bread and by some trick
she broke the ordinary loaf.

Pocket

it's better to sing it when it comes
because it goes again, or won't stay.
it's better to say, this heart is red
because it might not be, tomorrow
I ate the world, today I ate
an apple, dusk, complete
and downy where the calyx
withered to the inside of the fruit.

there's the platform your mind never left
or turned itself upside-down, the hut
painted on the bottom of the world
and the ground you needed a
crowbar to get into, but that's alright
these things take effort
you've got a certificate to prove it.

years later here I am, not your child
decidedly split from mystery
the one strand twists around everything.
across the middle of the night your daughter
doesn't talk about the dreams, the strange stories
and you did all you could, you survived.

there's someone else sprung in all of us
coiled up and waiting to walk away.
this doesn't mean much. I only know
your skin had spots, you were grim
before a camera

you died in a small town
smoked cigarettes, kept birds, plastic grapes
and carried a world, another world
there.

Summer Rain

in the event of rain
keep the earth still
or sleeping, so we walk

pattered
by the streamered air –
Oh, let us keep the earth still

and walk when nothing moves

but water and our water-borne limbs

Notes on Poems

'Lines' was written with Erica Kiely.

The Best of Montana's Short Fiction is the name of a book of short stories edited by William Ketteridge. The final lines of the poem are inspired by the story 'Blue waltz with coyotes' by Jeanne Dixon.

'Huntsman': *The Heart Is a Lonely Hunter* is the name of a novel by Carson McCullers.

'Wrecks': the italicised section is from 'Diving into the Wreck' by Adrienne Rich; in response to Alex Seton's work *Someone died trying to have a life like mine* at the Art Gallery of South Australia.

'Sisters': the italicised section is from the journal *Poetry*, Volume CXCVII Number 5 (2011).

'What the Crack Lets In' is in response to the Leonard Cohen song 'Anthem'.

'Learning To Love You More' is the name of a collaborative public art project archived at www.learningtoloveyoumore.com.

www.ingramcontent.com/pod-product-compliance
Lightning Source LLC
Chambersburg PA
CBHW062200100526
44589CB00014B/1880